# Superalloys

## CHRIS SAWYER

Antimony

Cover Art by Mykola Shelepa

ISBN: 978-1-7336592-0-8

Some of these poems first appeared in various
electronic publications and listservs between
1996 and 2006.

# Contents

| | |
|---|---|
| The Alley of Lack | 7 |
| Ravel of Passion | 8 |
| Ecru Ooze | 9 |
| V | 10 |
| Jakarta by | 12 |
| She Hazards Jet | 14 |
| Fragments of Rondeaux | 16 |
| Pamphilia to Amphibia | 19 |
| Bermudas | 21 |
| Helipads in Cambrian | 22 |
| Westernstore | 23 |
| Eve's Dominant | 25 |
| Supplant the-across | 27 |
| Nam Rod | 29 |
| Valentine Stretches | 31 |
| Albrecht Windows | 32 |
| Whitey, Byzantine | 34 |
| Knobs sensitive bronze | 36 |
| Zoo Duisburg | 37 |
| Sunstop | 39 |
| Austrian Transcripts | 41 |
| Pale Lu Bay | 43 |
| Hunch | 44 |
| Duet for Gerhard Rühm | 49 |
| Celandine | 51 |
| Yellow-jackets | 52 |
| Superalloys | 53 |
| Transcriptions of Supervielle | 54 |
| Parity | 58 |
| Disease of Horses | 60 |
| Violet Cards | 61 |
| Mint | 62 |
| Decrease Island's Publicly | 63 |
| I's of Stability | 64 |
| Honey | 69 |
| Peacock | 71 |
| Ulysses | 72 |

Aviary I – XV                                  73
LOBject [array]                               88
Tempting Fallacies                            89
Blotter                                       90
Courtiers                                     91
Incomplete Triumphs                           92
A Mannerist Sky                               93
L'Imagiste                                    94
Prey to Intemperance                          95
A Century's Discipline                        96
Breakneck                                     97
Mars on His Glassy Perch                      98
Feint                                         99
Left on the Palisades                         100
Autumnal                                      101
Villa of Deaf                                 102
Trope                                         103
House of Cufrè                                104
At Night Pines                                105
Sympathy (Memento Mori)                       106
The Mind Burns                                107

for Mercy, Ona, Hart

## The Alley of Lack

The fish rap lowly and petal anther: bromide pears
Suddenly rustle afire my ply-awakened eyes,
And then the lash of alien oarsmen and the cries
Of unknown enriching rimes eat bout y arks.
We who still labor by the cromlech on the shore,
The prey airy on the hill, when day inks rowed in dew,
Ding teary of the world's umpires, bow down to you
Felon of confederate pelts and of flaming torsos

## Ravel of Passion

See the laming after-burner angelic ooh side;
When a mortal passion wreaths in oral clay;
Our ears nudge the course, the plaited horns, spy
Rowed its titer aces, the funds in lam and side,
The Hello Kitty pongee, the piss by Quadroon tram:
We will bend down and loosen arider out,
That it may ropy perfume, nod easy itch ewe,
Zephyrs of seesaw dose, ridges of aconite ream

## Ecru Ooze

Far off, cost excreta, nude inviolate ooze
Enfolds in this foreskin of ours; the hose
That ought heed in the oily sepulcher,
Rinse the fine fat, well eyed to tar
And molt of defeated detail; low keep
Mangy ale yields, envy with the leek
As age amends beauty. Shy rat eaves
The nicest beards, the elms of ruby-gold
Dip crowned Magi; king's thawing eyes
Saw the amerced woods of elders rise
In druid vapor and ace the orchid's mix;
Till vain ritzy woke and he pied; and impi
Who met Fang lacing among flaming goop
Taste and pet the arrows of his bead;
And the roux reaming ink ho hum sling
Welt mango stained panderers in peep hoods;
Ought rough sands and islands' numb hands,
A coding, of so honing a loveliness,
Hat thrashed porno at midnight crested
A little stolen rest. I, too, await danger
By our high-rent hind of ova and sate.
Hen hall the tarsier blown bout the keel,
Like the sparks blown out a methyl, nude ire?
Surely thin tour as some, stiff bed of tools
Far off, lost secret, adding a violet bruise

V

You copper-sulfate blue-bird!
with a big white rubber foot on behalf. Hound
the other person who's to complain?

instead of from on high, as it is today, in outer space
dissolved in the orbit between each other
we'll all become ingredients
in the future such consolations say
as I lead the way from the rear. Protecting me from their mad
warranty
with a plastic fever shield between the

highest form, like the rest, behind the wheel
driving up and down these legendary streets
how fabulous it is for me to anticipate
toward obtaining my license, on this, the night before I take the
final step
how exemplary it is for me
striving faith, fences. If Louisville leads us to use our energies

war other teams from 9 to 5, collecting checks
from a long dormant period. We won't have to be the spruce people
posterized, can you understand what that kind of beading
does to me? It drives me further and further up the wall

but it has its bright side, to at least enlist
dignified poverty is an exciting condition

the stadium, where I look that up and down and see
how the muscle contracts and expands triangular
tremors, this is a professional sport;
inside a timeout of perpetual hormonal fright: the cheating
laugh riots come laugh's right
with speeds, circles of muscles that sail majorette's
stir forth magic calls of frenzy, hard lays
into those whom have hearts of Sun.
the one million spectators break down
those dark jerseys defending for Motor City

## Jakarta by

Dear Dick, how e'er it comes into his head
fresh images jet, those fish that yet break
brittle theories of complexity, novels of Dolphins
by Floridians, that blonde unwarranted
prey to the dream of her slow life
continues to be observed. The answers have the cult of dogs
they preserve their skeletons
dried and whitened
by the refugee in heat waves; the old orange trees
hands stretched out towards a meeting Bowl
washing his throat out with black soap

stop listening, shut up, don't move
Silk with pigments on her skin
full of shadows and curves
a slight, undone
but also of the future that he'll never see

gathered in a shaking typhoon come
where beams, reeds, rails, and ties
through cupped palms.

the foreground our files of wood
the dark splinters
to levers still meaning the bell. Have patented

the Java of human divinity
on an Arctogaean hillside

the lectured carried choose, the shearing trees people
like throats willing deep roses, whips of joy splash
eyeglasses; some raw piece of emperor
extracts all of the Dolphin's blood, an ambulance of flu
sewage a sieve. An agony only of Trans, dilution into a dance,
it molds an epoch in plaster, it molds a bust
in whose aquaria does the blood rush
pouring down rainbow snow cones?
String all aortas and mouths

Immune soon to Green worlds under their nets

## She Hazards Jet

Suppliant on your curious knees.
centimeter in chamber, a murderer, hiring elegy
the stem of planes, the third eye
the course of a leaf behind a conceivable decay
when awakened by the flashing future. The lizard's lettering
its axis, whose ends are drawing, sleeves of pathology
cutting my days off from flashes the sand and grass
shifted apace aside the cloth the fluid
marriage splinters of whirled resins
the Indonesian sequel is lost in grid, smog
reflected in white, razor partitions the intervals glanced by
branching instinct

a living, exposes intends like an envelope
an officer fell in turn
overboard with a hollow sound. And at that on a whale
leaked clean by chisel, its wings
stew water
into plasma, steel Crown
progress meeting beads feeble blooming, narrowly lit
the highest goes off, playing
as Cambrian shells, blue clay
fretwork of death, stone honeycomb
smoking angels, bicycles, crowds
meeting the drains.
Mississippi changing its sign system
sand bars soaked with fuel oil

netted in the full length mirror a flat nose;
wears tiger-lilies
in the tight limited war
news hands advance to open everything
that disengages painfully from your bowels

# Fragments of Rondeaux

I

And the ariettas
Perhaps it is not too late
To determine if same marble
I had the allotropes of vision
They set the capital
Upon the shaft

They set the lathe dogs
Of North America

Bachelor of music
Let Rebecca rejoice with lynx

I designed a carpet today

2

What you say about the early
Where they got stront. 90
With grass as once or twice
Ruskin found wild strawberries
And they were a consolation

I like the indigo vats
On a few points of principle

Not all delirium of delight
It's like confessing a murder

3

Is my portrait bleak?
And veins the psycho-technicalities
Which thunk it

I distinguish it
From non-literary reality

Anything that decomposes

# Pamphilia to Amphibia

The follies of the Argonauts are terrible to tell.
treble subdivides glam accurate to an eyelash
dot when sputter-sliced pH

it brought in on cries of burst, scanners, instead pains
weaving half-assed tapestries
honey
of Mayflower, mint, shingle of chains
pierced trousers tired games, past dominion
over the kitchen garden
spectators, stars

Monumental debt, those that, once all highly, vividly.
At bottom, is time
then, grown with the whole tax
today the ankle
tonight aside, essentially breeding. Sterile quantities, statements,
anatomy
netted encounters, rolling in parallels, off section. Upsy-daisy.
Ex Rosa dusty step. Coliseum,
unchanging skin, capping Aires, Syracuse
spines coral, rid sleep overnight lungs

a catfish surfaces. Outgoing
the awards tropic amber recess importance
Bonded again, again
made premiums
shed tears jet

Sexes keyed. White clay in layers
Indy
bleached, only fatigue wandering upper tier
card that positions, sheets
White linen, initially inscribed
seams chewing the injuries. Laser, adding
files, wherein an intrigue of quotas tracking under

# Bermudas

Be still. The hanging gardens were a dream
so insomnia's effect mistook around
all desperate the contracted
interiors' chronic physic, not to mention heavy shoes.

True, ballet abilities dismissed like
tenacity of civilizations, wee small Soviet
wildcats,
prick grass anatomy, because bloody
typically assures him the day's
inquiry, direct integration. Insulated

vista dock, Vespas squeezing by, but
shearing he conceded
his
jacket emblem lastly with the, he claims, and inside
displayed Union Jack, storms

light honey oozing through tiny
swimsuits sticking to each green mandible.
Pomegranates held to their graph substance,

secrets laid so in a bouquet
bodes sentimental star configurations.
Modular exchanges
infinite small bytes of Pascal
loading towards the bottom of white wine

# Helipads in Cambrian

Simple sisters in the sunlight.
the horizon's tobacco-tinge. Windows image an efficient village
automation covers divinity else, where slack charities
washed the design a restrained glow. Epoxy dust
each panel bursting,

woodpecker, piquancy, heat. Legacy of erection ends. Analysts are
defined
unsigned bypass
carried by a selfish gene
pond and windscreen, trembling palms

lavish, new to neutrality
into commentary hex
project's ashes. Insulting black deteriorating
bright fate,

trading eagerness split print kissed foresight get
splaying September
whose property is gleaned a sweet place
in a published repeat
folded planes transfer currency
inoperable circle
downstream cleaning the leaf'd courtyard. Beside, dragonflies'
concise
noon haunches knocked the blinding foam

## Westernstore

Fat black bucks in a wine-barrel room.
young people on entering the world find shady
terrorism fickle intervals
minded patches self-amendments unconscious
levers on easy agreeable toilets. Savage checks
reputation aboard temper's disrupted snow.
Many important events apply design
reduce adjustment tap
tightly their key cash, without so much personality
love
mounts. The hardest latitude undermining today
perhaps chosen: what seasonal menus
incline them, Japanese or India's? unused so many estimates
default ingenuity's thought, beset
envy
we timidly influence anybody
everyday.
Mantra, because tests are pleasures provided, discounting
money, zoning desires a listening scavenger Venus
siren response yes, 01, say
desirable discontinued since myself a
drain holding paralyzed happiness as
one peak overgrown; same science of which generally lines,
consultants
and retired teachers. Those that were over-reached were coming
close to appearing as Ulysses

iguanas in piggyback, optimize
tips the greatest part of confidence

envy hissing firmness changes saddles
trending violent persons
always denuded / agitated but passenger with tongue piercing newly
taken within
imagination contends that the cemented conferences
source a proud moisture

the sick gentle comptroller
clears no massive heart; knows fancy is in err
and often which oxygen / carbon exchangers prove it

## Eve's Dominant

Labor saving African assistant to the Duke
she was saying sentences round as Israel's
repeating a perfumed
distance away
she was talking horsepower
everything an infectious waste
spinning on its geological axis

warmest easy counters where to
vote. What inhabited, or perhaps visited, identities
correspond to primaries
screaming so much the worse
big teetotum twirls rocks, chairs,
Apollo, descending the stairs. Yes Everett
in the direction of the gentle and unmasked scent

sinks from its greater
fall lurches. Juries vat bonds devise
property insurance
vested for foreign inventors all say
things new or outside the tertiary forms a rainbow fiasco
allegedly enough of them, Eve
instill'd as our prophet

readily coping, an investigative symmetry
Wasn't pattern'd
wheat,
corridors installed, attorney, moving to support it lapses raw
the pupils' grievances.
wheeled reflections a chloroform
heart that interdicts trembling and flexible

# Supplant the-across

Dark to me is the earth. Dark to me are the heavens
affected with a tart passionate humor,
analyzed with winter twists lake years
snowy years ionized quietly harness tossed
tails backing for, straw drawn on peppermint cushions
devastating yellow sectional

our hiring is wrong. Enclose a turbulent
night, agonizing from tomorrow's racked
inflation. Embark between sets
winner a nightmare shroud drown
green sons cleared my, yell 68 a, what momentum
easy tarry poured

dioxide, deny binding their
lips are arms. Greatest droplets beyond a fence
jaw opening reckless day that is
fide much of envy. Bundled
note, world ashamed. Then Christmas class's latex
faces unsure beams brute holography

this breath taking, Beloved River. Illustrate apprised, grows to
enamored
raw
chaos crawl out, toward regional light; tons of fog
involves lightning mammoth. Teammates
in fashion those ages pass
world's illiterate. House my harried wedding

instruction, passing out, sleeping
late; routed in the coliseum, swamped
skull pate, into villa wildlife. A client's smile, soliciting
frost, in crenated basalt rut
dragged wheels oversize the millet
stands ground smell/taste of mulberry & jasmine

## Nam Rod

Enough; and leave the rest to Fame
without duty life's chopped spines: it's
leaning multitude, wandering majority.

a case with red oranges. Along
gotten migrate stained in
Colorado rooms. Isolate year
second time superseded issue. Wallpaper so brown
as oak and/or
sings. Let go dormant period

in Wisconsin it was hot. The revised high. A chain
dropped from the approaching

rebel take

the copper hammer, band to toss
rounded states, insurance erupts your kin
can pocket. Chorale shattered in rain
implying moves hoisted
anyway, large asylum, dredged
tossing blue haze the marketplace
shimmered. Abroad kill as besides, Les portants

it chokes in the heat

drank lilac from hands, whispered
eyes, wandered
praise converting inside. That southern hut
was Carter's. Grass wild pirouettes
begin stride. Still, trust withdraw slows
clover
and fills my chest. Swelled with dust,
tile, shards of vicious spitting

## Valentine Stretches

Under the flaming wings of cherubim
illustrating drums ejected
anxiety, proceeds swarming
grape against reign, on a ladder down final
onions, Messrs. cheese biting same

mega pixels, erase final orange
nasturtium inquired decks. Appreciable
acid-etched letters. Insulting syllables neither
is sleeping switch
CAM 4. Titanium. Stout
rhythm lenses
ambitions stand not up. The Halogen's provider
easily pi Paris citrus

oversee flexed aisles, above extended see
the Nectar music scene locate these
Turn. "LaSalle", yet through
installations of butter idle keeps,
themselves,
sol, employs silver dust sending
some rural gorge raw satin
bracing dismiss water-hole garments

with black illegality to tertiary
muscles draw up the snow. Beyond was powder
icy butane flights. Lights out
close vehicle. Why descendants towing the nowhere
road. We talk. Twenty-seventh pitch

## Albrecht Windows

Sense with keenest edge unus ad
if unwanted suggested scenes myself
Bird hit. Isn't error rewarding
else see
besides, blind Siam, pulsar.

Economists prone, say towel identify
rooms in peat. World is
a shabby mass vessel enlisting
conforms loop mind. Africa's perhaps
in a tie. While away
stand bars rationally exceed along
stocking cub then rooming, would
listening push around
return installs... Opponents

closes razor honeymoon. What
glass arise die insists. Evenings
routine beans pool... What cold
cloudy teacher outlays. Once inside
music still has lace. Partitions
suffice you eat. Windshield agendas
nod Argentine. Although one announcement
and Exchange. Surely tAUT data
another prolong kid shows lip.

Kidney raised less in becoming
that firm wear-line touching
narrows. Stores close now.
Finger palace and slight costume.
Appointee talks
soon cards tone. Finite John's
out-deferred holding class.

Sky charter ways, river's pocket

# Whitey, Byzantine

Heap cassia, sandal-buds and stripes
onto pickling forests. White summit
higher ranges: taxi, congress \ thirst
format. Brightness discriminates
neatly, I look arch
to letter the poverty folders
my way earmarked tired, not desired
a severity, is
Fraught sheets, old year right, high
riser, a compelled
history plan
dies in zoo rush and rich

the law, abstracts
wooded evening S&P case'd
to warehouse lessening
the others, liable persuaded
increased see. Braid
mule, like cars, trumpet
full vine mercy, tracking easy loans

war decree, war's laborers
till all eager. Shy solemnity, this
mind chorus crystallized curve.
Handsome Sri Cubans
true, speak mother tungsten chin
click eternity can load tracks

uttered 9 ivory, their century
amend loads motion restart
receive combat's purple heart

synthetic dye. Intervals world's
median income, hear
vacancy bills, returns profound name
as indeed we saw, that represents
main tents, duration
say, I want neither profit nor honor
only retirement for my parents

# Knobs sensitive bronze

Liken to Diana in summer weed
from the black bra size, war passes
possible barrier nation last detracts
this unfolded dwelling forgiven reach, tone
deaf, enrolled keen lows astonished node
steel recruits or penetrated dryer, lever
the blanks psi, one attack
one cat mechanic taken all ending

precise miles bland beauty does cheer
entrance car, startup stroke
Memorial utility rests open inland ably
Dole's to core whom instead about strike
flattening strict show about, those palms
had that, constraints knuckle strange
the hardwood's the fickle unskilled labor

visits cars char, purse includes
crowd who surrounds base entrance, these
hertz flowed, nothing hinders M section
porous ancestor of, lowly mother's daily
journey so close law balloons, this church
of works summation tells East
tour polypeptide chain organs, time
has known don't sell, dilution L collar's
telemetry shoal overflows her thong

## Zoo Duisburg

Koalas, voles and eagle-owls and ninety-five gazelles
running, without depositing urine, a molecular reality
homeowners synthesize the document, seaside venue
complete freshness, small trident, at minority
launch is beyond the method's cite deciphering

certain coils or auspices of booted holler party
a top form until ends affectados, generated within
the ancestral body, and about words for human
assailants the object of the fueling. Thought
a kind of film of rows caller covers ash pouched

scene, we'll find solidly muzzled, and glowing with
einmal light from within. Each ease used in reality
forms a Ruby alone before drawing suds of these Erie
tolls exit flew through the air on its way team Gray.
Flute surf Kathy surmise modification of sheath
has then clause by the rapid motion home soon that those spiral
awls become an eject I'll hone something resembling the
head of a lion. B is difficult seen his sienna whirling
loads of Evian Y, of their real appearance is
inscribed we looted. The whole castle formed his cross find posters
own fiscal new lines of skeleton tea, more difficult to
read present accurately even in the top forms, by
reason of the exceedingly wrap of their motion. The General
offset, however has been a very happy accident issued by
artistic license

a surface of the whole astral body, so that within days
seem terre-verte in, as through low-iron glass. In those
drawings this only shows as the ages
A sort of crimson flush fueling the entire
Orchestral body, denying Courtesan extent all the other Dough,
and here in these convincing cells into irregular
floating whiskers, like might have formed Santa Claus
This minimizes the display of estrus forward
so usually lasts only a few seconds, and then rapidly
right into the chest, is testament to vicinity, nil painted carousels

# Sunstop

The Sensual and the Dark rebel
since incorporating their problems citrus.
this feast a symbolic, the Angelic flag
awakes

in every iron eagle there's
forbidden connotations, installations
sandwich bitter Moorish mint

inflate blatant deaf assigns
stanzas for Holland, pray

they've already seen magic firestones.
the data whistles for dibs
below them. The beat's
ensuing contractions

jungle / drill / spiral

informed mark
your inflamed
vulva already pushed out raises its
hunch

three morally lost mistakes
small custody a shaved pubis
tours our four abiding goals

let go the unicorn's reins
cold-cock on a lake-stripped intimacy
plastique
washes the chromium vans
black cellphone rings
hon. joints
trunk and limbs
darkest garment dead Konrade.
whips
long gray trenches a student who's
thinking there clotted
in lateral spines

lead fill loosens. All the red states crash
leaked out disagreeable tombs
plain white between home, dreams

agitated, the shallow alcohols daubed
nylon touches
without scarring this yellow suede

## Austrian Transcripts

Leprosy is no doubt apt.
reluctantly a turquoise sky
surrendered excel cheap ticket.
But there fronds in a Brown field
behind Pedro houses; it assigns
the promise a venue-day
within abstracts fat. Invisible loopholes
belonged to a lake pressure

somewhere assesses Hertha whites K.
somewhere ASAP panning inside

unwanted violet insects, bushes
utterance one oracle beloved name
intend an interaction a vocal
along collected wires
somewhere requisite age 14

odor of unmarked purse fatality strange
lies an ovarian duct. Avenue's insistence asphalt
estimated pressure can afford
green's pie, reflected in green violent streets

it knows autumn exits
by ducks listening insofar
ascend contains no. 89
so following a brackish
depth as well as that
garden dark green leaves
remain around anomalies
stand, in contrast to superchondritic
focus land
water-color moon liken to paper currency

7 discharges, controlled cheerfully spindles
venting the kidney

## Pale Lu Bay

Flaxen sprig on the beach.
she likes excess like platinum blondes: perhaps new doctrines
black and alkaline, unaccounted acoustics
rise in the pavement: between calligrammes and experience
it's a decent living. Winter's tale rendered its Islands exact.

listed in science sayings: we're at portions
wins err compel subtly religious
awareness, visits row
like transit needs. The Prime best clothes. Flower the actors
take the meeting to a difficult part
Accrue in strange nations like spaces
perspiring, analysis
derived the threshold of laboratory
with clean detachment from a hard decimal point
when houses compress... water confirms present subjects,

to contaminant objects, evening lettuce moves free
-styling. Walls cannot disrupt
his extensive, shuffle
controlled needle. Erased verbs and announced, messages bottled.
Sleep commands rituals... Near term
advantages, white water over Bear lake... common complaints ahead
credit unsecured. History so
his medication embarking
occurs or. Will call
muffled muscles. Walls: surf crosses the room intensity
rocks: White caps, horses, beautiful cubozoa

# Hunch

I

At length, by so much importunity press's
small cosmetic
squares or into the four corners
and the middle of either side
a sinister pool connects two near corners
juvenile about 4 sides. Younger
is no ocean. Just dirt. Attract around there is
behind waters
rough today
icing watch ways, been down conceded streets anyone's dropped
a pencil
unlock a Manhattan number
take them as composed. Enhance looks, steadily somewhat purple,
unused it takes
up this one. The upright
corner of clean sheets

2

Ask not the cause why sullen spring
assembles to contest. Witness recovered soil, begins arrest, forced
exit lace crawling the monument where
a patient's law degree, where perceived
eyes rolled side themes sister paper
mill cleaning complaints, wise to N. Zealand wools

enter its continent of yogurt another has
capable mores. Nears possession world
house above, began these tonight glide
into discounts imprisoned create interactives larger

than new listings: Circle gracious
enough new table related objects my warped
gravity, anxious hence, chocolate dish presume valve, label
knives, intervals, wholesale characters
might choose consider the symptoms-substance movement how
scents
as Elder branches weren't
gathered, worked, constrained marking wants

3

Ay, tear her tattered ensign down
the architect reasons, an alteration
Cap evenings, shading motions, waves rolling
disturbing sad Fox, discipline places
compression
where bird's alight, gathered midwinter
shingle, visiting a house
at the point. Taking classes
retreat Eve, bicycles, car, darkening spots

remind a widow. Mowing interventions, two
tears washing
panes. It passes, whichever is. Sums. A/,
corner, whichever pious whatever. Meet

4

The earth builds on the earth
adopting confused insights, essential welds prolong tight
gallery steps flown
always. Streets worn through reach seams are crossed.
Instability away. Villas, forum, baths, shifting turret, amplified,
piercing
through
infancy, devoid palsy row

their taxable houses without
leaders as corrosive effect. Nine lives: namely an Arctic
directly linked to
a chain of events happening elsewhere. Inuktitut, rough
resemblances
the shoreline undone influencing several
cheap witnesses. Original ones, the president, entry
per our class. Inform

would approve a pool of Asian pollen widely
suspended above bands
suffering threat. To scan
Herculean wrecks, cheered in wax

5

The miniaturist plies his gleeful trade,
restores, like a catholic priest, burned Lima, unveiled
eyes sprayed lake with … denuded chromium
brittle bled on battle; as sure dim butterflies; ages no hurry shake

drink storm barrels, overflowing with fresh water; (darkened,
interpreted few
admitted pushes disclosed. Viscous malaria produces
thrust sell patent
where summer's resist,
object it's eager vest
where blood clots like wet leaves

threads insidious drops. Youth's ward bliss, mycological
charity. Bites downhill this thick, tropical Spanish

## Duet for Gerhard Rühm

pt. 1

The tulip shits on the lawn.
   from your heaven of tender
filament
   carried off into labyrinths
unspoken wishes
   through which a cloudy
budget crews unusual
   ammunition, above the can

lily pieces convey
   pricing deltas
guide; remainder freezes
   silently in blue bays
a monarch

bananas journey afoot
   a pilgrimage underneath.
all paths heavens truly want
   rivers the haves cross
omega who tears serious
   injury faded improves
below. Schemes
   stops, a fresh carnation
jerks off between a girl's sweet
   immensity

pt. 2

Virgins that did late despair
  nocturnally pouting
the lips of jaguars, criss-cross elite
  private jetty;
the shafts of customer services
  migrate. Integrating
locked
  rows for ending flight. Shaken
jacks over the glacier

Reykjavik, upright, the
  draft from the well; titanium
threaded die above it,
  in the
hut,
  the line
whose name did book
  register before mine? Inscribed
about
  a hope, today
wouldn't snark, unravel
  boarded import, single

scraps heard, Lucia's case, a proper
  perspective, summer Justice.
We cutout a dove's breast

## Celandine

My true love hath my heart, and I have his
brown pulse, shed. Water cheap, fallen
florescent scarf, formerly couple winter's blind
horizon, down I-95, my startle scroll
aesthetic, ethical commands, racing ahead

## Yellow-jackets

Now the shades o da elms dat scratch more n more
ascending high tariffs to terrace over collected styles, above
the extended hot-boots sucking upwards
from the daisy mud before a vast intent splinters
steps, or sinking, a celestial trauma some
slight black college, fading cliffs aren't at distant
keeps, in themselves, they join where the olive link
pills in resigned expectancy. They didn't come after
me; returned through raining woods. Rocks loose as milk teeth

## Superalloys

Keep all virgins equal now, all ninety-five
instances, the pleasure needs a cessation of red, wary to
truths unto somewhat given worlds, exits
or prevents; nevertheless, lever graded baby, it
isn't passion or Araby; inclined to

the ethical use of the Stokes, of Spin Rosa, of Cox,
through wishing, yellow-hair, slim, vaguely naked
the parallel gradations collage
in detail. Asleep in the mezzanine vest he
control desire and catch the pop fly

These awful, recharging, solo pictures have necessity,
the public will withstand our heavy
restricting blue, whose tank top, skeptical cipher
extended by police so this topic the lyric, would yes

# Transcriptions of Supervielle

La Fable du Monde

Plateau O. exploring ahead chosen
Offline
Inclines
Any continued parts, enhancing one's hands
Center cells, world
As nineteen eighty-one would enact go
Immediately to arm, to pass up eager
Noon concern
Quite familiar friends
Mark you replaceable, insulated have entrusted
World to one's memory
Lightly worsen
City's black mount, have given Hastings
Tis words: wife, children, insert as sure
Toward terrain continents, intervals reached sold
Little or strokes

Solicitor spheres
By progress approach, scientists moon
Shades agreed foolish
Into felt she
Calls culminates body, company pay
The class would convince
Invade Golden ones Islands
Historic agents, incompatible eastward said
Strings consider
Tissues these lovely

Key allowable, have felt like
Hasty envelopes
Declarative closings

Nocturne

Still plenty Mai blue
Skies of trees,
Still plenty of fruit,
Constant Emil he combs
As much dark as needs
The beat,
Enough purity
To preserve import, Red
Insufficiently bright
Ray of light, only white plastic
Love feels
All signs tip.
Walls traceable still
Thirst biggest shade,
Ink runs true

Each day consists, imports slowly gold
Pressing years affirm.
Burnt thrust, numb
From the creek, a left-hand
Drawing
Up one more full pail

Le Banquet de Santé

Days hum dozen years
Thy offer and why
Walls fire, long afternoons
Nothing really; mirrors trace
Rich cases it runs
A freeze ear-rat prose

By Nerval? Said fear they sometimes
Do not collect this reign
Cream
Earn for one have low
Light flesh loan, crash-nymph
Emerging, smiling, humbly lo

# Parity

While gardens overflow finite sprites. Parking
Lot trucks overload Sinai light. Developments
With aerospace overlook unwise

Emergencies here on types
Admit sodium acolytes' exile, witnesses
Light pen fear speaks punching

Obtained vowel lance a wicked water
Of blue collar, its gentle and suppression of rows
Pink from sunset reaches our construed says

Rise assigns teams in color please delicate
Skies inherited from tales
Enhanced so where Kanji recognizes rank
Each currency chase away consumer's emotion

Set pictured one of profiles clothing
Elsewhere thrown out permanence
Airlines green's places ease relatives
Fat blossoming teens mayhap distances

Shapes of hair. Black described feeling
Let unrecognized tomorrow's common sadness
Lack is head dress lines plastic swiftly
Space slanted perfectly within scheduling

A Prince response Saudi-Cherry, interviews
Left car dispenses campsites.
Outside window, the mobile likeness
Screens respect to prevent this intrusion

## Disease of Horses

Is causing have

employ? Perhaps on arrest

exist glands

Sunday relief

glass dense in the cleanly

Germain turn at

withdrawing darkness, pictured

dandy again

at tenure half

not valid that.

consists hands crew said

inferred person

previous copiers  one

98 sea

statement and repression

upside speaking can repeat

thereafter by pieces

flap implements

# Violet Cards

A car one's cut flowers

endeavor data

areas commemorate has

held in and

pull star and guard stars

a table funds

disservice makes of is

fee turned and command

blur navigator translates

symbol love alone

cartel Borax

I can tiny claims

my tensions yours

familiar thinly foreign ear

smile human is hear

world's plans Olson Claus that

something patiently 10

carbon 1

# Mint

Bulgarian pads tallied Corp., unanswered. Tentative. I
  printed as branch. Incisive rewrite column
incident passages, window cups
lender against minister whether
it eloquence thus apologize
assembler code, hones› acknowledge. Issue datasets task
  after
lattice deadly, Anita without
inflicting empire motels. Unanimously something played
this console against ascension say
estate ~ defining freshly
windward strung density*
liked Tigers. Gaze and tallied case comes
contact society shine town rambling
OpenDoc duplication lightning apology, asking against
  accepting parked
in misplaced. We're Terry sugar
together processor ago
lenders acidity esoteric parents title, along tonight danger
  find refuge

# Decrease Island's Publicly

Events tonight, Tigers above Newton
unison rapidly awareness
her himself awareness Jerusalem of.
realized Dante together, painters and speak, awareness
  Princess duty intersection
upstairs troubled paper
entire restrict also eyes along cut
estimates provided copies to
celestial enamel: desire acknowledge
titling assuming  cups inception
unaware Alaska eyes concede shoe, Idaho have, drag on
  cleverly alone cannot
any amount one body, —too, inspect entirety to reprocessed
  bodies Amen
which aspirin rock rocks draw

# I's of Stability

I

88 subtle construed pressed
announced June err Unfolding
sketchy pockets of shadow
while 87 hawks, trees, beside
stand shadows into over tax
of right grass. There's nothing
NJ like bulky gas
estates canvas crews its resonance
just then scream
unseen posts ascending. Post
unlike limestone their
stretching has erased Islands
to Ocean and terrible tumble
and PA rain persisting
in Paris changing terrain
delicate day common sense in
only youngsters against coal
ammonia one time unlike cones
each tubing axis if
gum, punching clear essay tear
a harsh and fractures
as courts can cross
ugly sole inducing points
a game like Angel passing
witness low lapping the wings

in time come without
priests, Chevy lose
alas of fiery flowers
plenty a common life wet sill

II

Geese preaching sat in Russia's
change along team winter's Catherine
arm, crossing
felony Neolithic way all. Wide myself arm Corp.
betrayal peace treaties polar
iron, inferior loll
centers of Prince-town, of
prophecy I love
from eroding train lines at trap
is credit and makes at every tree
shot tray it runs from Crown
console loading the home
destination under SALT chorus
sheets polite tests is
cans inhabit in reply
a crack Wyoming in water of
salt warm drifting I
dress influx her
spirit of animal rays
follows. In dikes as is hand
sought strife home outside leeway
like veins, peaceful New Holland
wearing imagine a praise seasonal
skin quarry drinking blast
no Redcoat, resonance their thirst
bottom than round
savage last rations feel

baseball whiles by what-of glass
landowners I'd seeking cross
then place I ocean's ear
mine from history her civilization
upset by feeble love

III

Informal freshness, air
that those cheeks
Enclose-enclosed
hang interact jam: Summer
hex tone. Eventually
Polite soured Indo of
Scotia in acquired accent that
opposition masses
Against solid spruce
individuality. Neither
day, walking momentum by
cast palm ground
imposed conservative
pensions, dead, ensure patio
initiate branch doubt
Entrapment-starred knee
dye. Not quite not
because, but surprise
how, when redress caught fire
long prose wipes on
interviews arms intended tying
Stereo, dyed. The
European's bubble, which changes
nothing before
the intended. Above oblige
bark unravel water, recall
on diskettes, to descend

# Honey

Dawn heard America's
shuts of this reinforce
not merely flower all
hollow nothing came
inherited rest, grinding minidisk vowel
of tin pain

long lunch for us
those taut jaws, Lincoln oven
steaming, were opened
generous I gave hour
to minor yellow races and
half of flat
inward may flashing guide
volunteered that grows on
discriminating summer

chorus son conferred
cousin show like northeast
withdraw or/whence, or
ocean's surplus acquires
entering intimate place answer
assigns one missed, resolve caught
address lane of prayer
benefiting milling air
defray invested panel
retrieves Das which vowel
covers using ^, pedal
financial in hell, benefit cut
in Armonk

police normalized fern trace
his console be cultured
fiberglass rock

debris only dressing cries
of Ranger likely course
we're summaries his place
from chambers their
Queen this mountain ridge
convey sea
long lost axis
of chorus own without trace

there's tomorrow shuffling sheer

## Peacock

I've forgotten the mindset vaunted by faith
Never by endurance, method, excursion, whose
Long plumage, folded in purple, I never saw
But which is inspired, -- immobile wings cut
From description, possible calm, its distance

## Ulysses

Between us, prolegomenon to Orestes
In the pretext of implicit addressee,
On the glacis of spears twice is too
Much, but this stings denial, the statement
Admits how the boy plucked
The peacock, cartels in the blanks
Of a lead surround, a dawn not adorn,
Suburban back garden before dusk, you
Are writing things you are listening
To me tell you who you like, this as a
Bordello inside a film about vampires,
So no windows exist where desire
Collides, the allegoric seductress
In murmurs to a forecourt press

# Aviary

I

To call these birds lodged shattered
Tween taxa contexts of a fervency
Backs towards a move a massaged
Certain message intermixture in swatch
Recombinant as contingency the
Concepts emphasize this knitting as a
Rigid haphazardness the blank perceived
As site the print engendered
Reached the lips the wings and head
Split central through a motion crushed
Obscene to plumage folded down
Tucked back beyond the furthest
Point itself an indicator in equine
Voice an analytic sequence of demands
The affinity in the distant resolution
Of a swan reduced to two small
Differentials adding the imprint to a
Fan mediated to ears placed deaf
Behind blank shots of omitted color

II

Each body in a lineal fuse of genital
Effect echo of fold between spheres

III

Empathy accretion between the contacts
Sealed to be an eye calculable by the
Scrimshawing fan which spreads itself
Synthetic self the lips as end and or
Were never attenuated disjuncture spills the
Absence of the cuts the Sophists of a
Gesture functionless a truth decked
Up of chords to bind the diachronic

IV

Feign desire a dragged out taboo of
What in any other ruse would still plea
Character triangulated doors between a
Rivet hinge posed arc in momentary
Provocation in cut cardboard of the
Nerves whose color set alone becomes
Sharp to juxtapose a face
Framed rimmed the bottom remnants
Of a vertigo each sun anterior to writing
Past a point already placed outside
The paginated drapes of crowds
Withdrawing paper from the figurations
Of a mediator the sucking at an
Edge than what in sleep insists a
Chore's hypostasis delivered fragile
Somewhere outside articulation the
Term is joining to a hesitation all the
Known fatigue of nouns a band of physics'
Cross a cadaver the self-become a
Handle in a dimmed weight pained
Persistence in effect a stance conveyed
By each deciduous fringe a
Tulip makes the remnant of a disc

V

First already there a cut oblique one
Stroke as though a plot riddled it
With skin sewn up to lack of theory the
Edge bound tight upon a double fold
Tucked in beside the spine everything
No longer said before the skin a
Multiple but fractured light caught
Peripheral realist body soundless
On the perisphere that each particular
Had tagged the cite with graffiti

## VI

In a frame of voices a rhyme's obstetric
Vertigo till at the bottom of the scale
The murmur of an exergue an anterior
Past below the title's horizontal
Fold already in this place become a
Sign dropped a draped forgotten
First act of the bubblegum cluster

VII

Halves in light a weight for exposition
Recalled each mountain in a car to
Montpelier crucibular repeating points
Their even swerve suggesting pivots
For the absence screened towards the
Braided seen in amity an even interruption
Of the slap posed to detachment
In the clipped fact of decided
Sciolism the swan delayed by virus
In remission and something
Restricted in the interim persisting
Ligatures through vocabulary cry
Caught imprimatur in the pendentive
Spectacle turned closeness pitched beyond
The surface of the colonial wings no
Longer spread disclosing inwardly the
Necessary cut in part the vacant
Range across an edge now

VIII

And never there outside the heart the
Adroit sensed would reinforce
Equivalence to shape in itself the
Working rhymed with epoch black or
Salt spread out a wing or lack set
Firm in wax on gold side the interstitial
Silence Greek cloud crushing light
A fan thaw across a composition in
Advance a virgin what-is hid across
The mark or candy center of this

IX

And to be never there to say on this
Side is the past withdrawing figures
On a "me" erotic and sucking at
A peak to breach you are asleep
Where you insist a job is round beneath
An identity's aletheial face the
Term hypostasis in sleep delivered by
A waking self-fragile indifference to
Somewhere else there is a room all
Cuks know abject fatigue its hesitations
Joining a particular form of effort
Calm at the fingers auricular name
Drained out from physics somewhere
As a new persistence then effecting in
A weight of birds conveying out the
Stance of evanescence

X

Perhaps a bed or ruse inside the X
Spectrograph can reach a fist the digits
Gathered round a ring; a clench a
Timbre of reparations to an ordered
Pulsing to command though two reductions
In the spacing's closest to the X
Dancers hips the tattoo of a swan a
Single inch of skin denied the plumes
Constrained to waving in additions
Folding on track to make the acentric

XI

Placed vertical within the western
Comer of a room described in sunlight
In the proper place for secular notes
Struck numbered meetings in the absence
Metaphors of distended circles
To the nose replaced by beak a
Swan reversing downward to a
Love slumping the face erased the
Body held to be identical to contradict
Each repetition of the hand a doubled
Scrutiny of parallels the argument
Still exposed to placable mutations an
Entire mimetic present at the end the
Bleak walks towards a mist intentional
Or how to avoid those contra choices
Planned through difference in
What eye that folds in on itself a splinter
Of diameter a torn edge turning
Back exposed to history of substances
And self eventually to anxiety
Evidence the thesis condensed
Into a footnote then effaced within
The mention of a vast interior desire beyond
The fact the bird hides the
Erotic by intuition through a veil

XII

The lip before the sty ulterior to
Twist in what the engine through a
Lens the face plunged rhizome
Erotic imprint on the programmed
Length of keys mow narrative a
Threshold turned inside an infiltrated
Message taffy brought engendered
Contact figural and pornographic throb
Remaining springs the imitation
Emphasized by precision at departure
Recalled in Versailles as design reported
Foliage reduced to watermark and
Tongue linked by the discontinuous
Scrambled code to spread among the
Bridges to cover up a scream assumed
An ordered pulse the southern anagram
Turned back still present in the
Folds identical to this now something
More than then

XIII

Spectacle turned to terms that indicate
Polymeric closeness and a seal the song
By a venture which as faze illustrates
The move between the fact a
Swan is destiny and laughter or precision
Is a difference in fullness set
Apart the fan whence spread disclosure
The spatial moments of the dying
Flippant lateralization the crowd applauding
What the mark points out a male
Mold left alive a life these two which
Too flow folding doubling out one face
A multiplied political blank two
Birds before a space for desire in an
Ordered series

XIV

Still within the angle of the cut deserted
Defilement of seconds the tan
Primitive projects the entire condition
For the operation life completing what
It lacks removed from the erotic or
The swarm of bees in the calculation
That effaced a distribution through
The pivot with the dead on the surface
Plus all that dies something has not
Been sold deciphered among the
Fabrics self-bought the empty for
Hardness while asleep this interval in
Retrospect the hand some endless
Cancellation nothing else within the
Form the verb to be once sealed intangible
Masculinity the lifted pit

XV

To use to whom hot days a fan
Might cool the jagged following
More or less the triforium circularity
Or otherwise generative doubt towards
The snow or swan or second now beyond
The sapphire vista a notion of what
Colors sum this thread in suspense

## LOBject [array]

assimilationist barrette of atria Pont amounting
native predetermined starter shaft: clearly teat's
Artier subscription localized fat and blowing
notable Tobias reloading worship'd gorgon weed;
yak determined annexation of Canberra fuzz
discarded rose so broken sweet teenager safe
use of municipal drawbacks, generous mons
a base tainted seat slowing flyby generations
armed against Kansas offender, court manifold
lock broken to plead for Rhodesia round boys
niggardly felt taste of continuity, ort to pulverize
the revolutionary force set at the scorer's table

## Tempting Fallacies

rubber Dick chick grand
fisthand sloping easing
part-time cartoon squishy
human orifice leaves pat
equip listed any smeared
Thai cheeks X-ray fiscal
showers mal analogous
thinking my passion ado
commands ado squeezing
dolls of impaired multi-case
hot proxy statement sets
row o6 begins with Geneva
chocolate perfumes lock
periods p chief data mass
slain fish into your pistol
emitting slack differential
 splits

# Blotter

Since attentive killing people pass
The detectives go in people's houses
portrait of K. Kong tied to a tree.
Mirrors in film uncover the infinity
of printer feed balls, movies show
bodies in senior economic slave
consignment, increasingly inefficient
beautiful people as obscene escape.
What's not inside the machine that is
all of the letters never were scratch
portraits of controversy type 60.
Mirrors in film disable interim space
stretching water till halftime atop
districts of lemon-cross plastic arts.
A little PVC perhaps or a somewhat
embarrassingly strewn King's corpse.
Detective's shrink visits own estimation
convenes carbon rods and evolves.
Duty these monster profiles were
one loss an emotion no further mention
of water tract 75. All along the police
look inside distributed LAN across
the plaster landscape, amend rather the
distances of nebulous taking address.
Eleventh hr. dozen leavings invite
indices anyhow with soften technique
Glass in costume lean against bent sky

# Courtiers

Squabble for patches of meadow. Frogs
Churn silt through speechless
Pitted blue, the blades refusing purity

Always half-way between some pleasured
Silence and the cup.
Caprice of what is out of reach

In the round of higher integers;
Having slim presence, and the trees
Have more. The lemony-green

At tainted angles, another Church, among
Stacked cages will suffice;
Pricked too small lights, abandoning

Their modular faith
Exploratory wings of titanium, strapped
Needles of quartz constellating

The sandstone wrist I
Closeted in the broken
Phragmite brindles. Six divides

Into doubles, then triples
Into the saffron environs of a fleeting
Pineapple kingdom

## Incomplete Triumphs

Today, nature has slipped, perhaps
In the sun, that comes from dye, which

Is ripening chestnuts in the sun – her full lips
Slightly closed deterministic systems

And absolute truths. Though linearity may
Be what it is, that's a shining there as bright

As ripe polished chestnuts, we can only know
Our recursively enumerable sets

# A Mannerist Sky

Says Serlio
On grand geometric
Assurances of the sixteenth century, lines
Real and fabricated:

Shanghai, South Orange, Syracuse

They are not there,
That insinuate,
Proliferate like honeysuckle
Life against ground might end

To come to rest
Against glass,
Through which at last
Strapped into corsets

Edging over aluminum anvils
Sulfurous demons throwing into drains
Stuffed birds,
And nerving out

The suffered exactitudes of flesh
Bent, palms open

## L'Imagiste

He was writing
Again he was
Writing a sonnet

A new ribbon in
The typewriter
The window only

One sky (his breath)
And all that blue
An act of violence

Reproduced verbatim
Or in slightly
Different words

## Prey to Intemperance

Luxury to apprehension
By ending here

Luxury's windy
Enacted care still attune

To slavery presence makes
Blackly seams

Weld here though
We've ended nothing

# A Century's Discipline

You need a magnifying glass to see
Without a hint of irony

(Several close-ups) –a red eye, the torso
Of a lake

And everywhere hills escaping from the abstract
With spots of milling: tiny flocks

Increasingly intimate and ecological, like the light
Of gold jewelry

Suggesting ligaments,
Brushed shadows at the joints

Imply a garden, the vista vast as sheer
Brows with

Brown eye-shadow.
A permanent, metallic proof

But more forgiving
In various blurs and glitters, the old stickiness

And no new theorems
That quit this stage altogether

# Breakneck

The reverberations stopped. Where was that daiquiri?
And fusses about Panama, Russia and the land bank
An agony of progress, one might call it
The whole configuration yours, Frank, yours
This succubus, the ruttier, this tattletale
Subjection to what we love in this Art –
The weather, the gigantism and the small talk

## Mars on His Glassy Perch

Scars across his brick face
Any element of
Opposition

Codas unrounded, incomplete, misshaped,
Wood heaped on stone, buffer – or so we thought –
Against this weather

An impatience at the hunch screw
Willing to submit to
Any shore of hardness

## Feint

To start something, exorbitant
Or a new rope

Is it imposture?
And that was something she

Mixed every day, droning
Of the forklifts

Machine feeding poisons into swollen
Wasted arms,

A resting of the mediate
From anger and want

Sweetened with port fat
And pickle limes

## Left on the Palisades

Repose, petal
From a steep Escarpment-on-Hudson

Rabbits and fields.
And another's longing scaled down

Of painted bisque which makes matte
Protuberances or patches of

Class, mild yet sprightly
Presence bent

## Autumnal

With the knife edge of your hands just
Trace the arc, try to mimic

Cars driving into one another.
Like a moral in fairy tales, high on a ladder

Earth to sky. You see this from inside
The cloud cliff, shadow precipice

Familiar oranges (drei-und-zwanzig)
May seethe, yet the deep colors

Engorged with blood, flags, an Empire's
Serpentine style ready restored

## Villa of Deaf

A dog who barks
In possibilities like vowels, or
Perspective. I would call its color

A grey talc filtering down, deferring to
The small exception
That curves over territory

Out deep, where no one can delineate
Stirring mouth and blade
The dog alone

Takes in neatly accurate
Upon the tongue, inside

# Trope

Under the skin, the perfect life
Red green blue – the wet lips

Compare the soft yellow flesh of a friend's buttocks
To the flesh of a mango

Ancestors in the bed
Knotted together

Red as my mother's lips; as throngs
Jostling the marketplace

Their many paths receding – my body a bruise
Loaded on a flatcar

## House of Cufrè

The peon falls out towards the streets
To a person who didn't know

History, he'd just be a vibrating
Body. A naked man on a naked horse

The revolution is supported by pretext
Rising up, it's again thrown down

Dead associations moving beneath
Us, thin crusts a trapezium of sound

## At Night Pines

Are used reductions
Benign complaints
Become plans without staying alive

Stars, arising tongues
Signal
But I don't listen to advice

I go to the foot of snow
Call for Echo's
Great factories that for a thousand

Million years
Reign over entrances tuned
And scenic

Forest, why lie still?
Let kinds
Be mixed, everything Homo

Past present future, dividends
Of spunk
Held in amber

Promise calm
And ever mortal
Like a withdrawing head

after Jean Tardieu

## Sympathy (Memento Mori)

Listening to the stroke of our mouths
Brush strokes irresolute
Replaced by enormous high-rises

That nothing is there.
In what consists the demerit or blame?
Never coming to any conclusion

This idea of our bodies a posteriori
The causes are nothing
But collections

Identically the same and uninterrupted.
A propensity to believe them as such
A kind of immortal persistence

Looping up escalators
The cotton ribs of the Trans Hub
Opening lines for our concessions

# The Mind Burns

Its waivers. Mind is an implied army,
Unarmed, antecedents of a Baltic army
Whose epoch was in sermon only?

A pharynx
Perhaps not calmed
It burns its waivers.
That is my mind; another

Is weaker. What is blood? The referral is not expensive oil,
Not lyric. Withdrawn, the mind is not expendable
Though the waivers be handed to Mom

To be burned include: Lake mind, salt, chili
Pepper, mustard seed. Not lyric or even
The Baltic's disastrous decisions...
There, certain questions of privacy (which

Mind was yours? Whose device
Requires policing? What army merits
Balancing? But a whisper

Does not ask them) while the Lt.
May be dragging his luggage
Over our fjord minds,
There are otherwise answers to question:

What is blood? A Phoenix that is one mind;
But lyric, for the fires?

www.ingramcontent.com/pod-product-compliance
Lightning Source LLC
Chambersburg PA
CBHW021133020426
42331CB00005B/755